Do giant pandas have cereal for breakfast?

Written by Katie Foufouti
Illustrated by Nathalie Ortega

Collins

What's in this book?

Listen and say

giant panda

cereal

breakfast

In the morning, Giant pandas eat bamboo for breakfast. They love bamboo!

bamboo

After breakfast, I brush my teeth.

Then I put on my shoes and my jacket.

Then I walk to school.
What do giant pandas do after breakfast?

After breakfast, giant pandas go
to sleep. They like sleeping in trees.

At school, I learn new things every day.

At playtime, I play games with
my friends.

I love playing! Do giant pandas play games?

Giant pandas like sleeping, but they like playing, too.

climbing

They like rolling on the floor and climbing trees.

rolling

We have lunch at school.

Today, we're having fish, potatoes and peas. What do giant pandas have for lunch?

Giant pandas eat bamboo for
lunch, too! Bamboo is good for them.

In the afternoon, I go home and I play with my sister.

Then we have dinner.

After dinner, I go to bed.
Where do giant pandas sleep?

At night, giant pandas sleep in trees.
Goodnight!

Picture dictionary

Listen and repeat

morning

afternoon

night

breakfast

lunch

dinner

brush teeth

walk to school

play games

put on

1 Look and match

rolling   climbing   eating

sleeping   playing

2 Listen and say

Collins

Published by Collins
An imprint of HarperCollins*Publishers*
Westerhill Road
Bishopbriggs
Glasgow
G64 2QT

HarperCollins*Publishers*
1st Floor, Watermarque Building
Ringsend Road
Dublin 4
Ireland

William Collins' dream of knowledge for all began with the publication of his first book in 1819.

A self-educated mill worker, he not only enriched millions of lives, but also founded a flourishing publishing house. Today, staying true to this spirit, Collins books are packed with inspiration, innovation and practical expertise. They place you at the centre of a world of possibility and give you exactly what you need to explore it.

© HarperCollins*Publishers* Limited 2020

10 9 8 7 6 5 4 3

ISBN 978-0-00-839784-5

Collins® and COBUILD® are registered trademarks of HarperCollins*Publishers* Limited

www.collins.co.uk/elt

British Library Cataloguing in Publication Data

A catalogue record for this publication is available from the British Library.

Printed and bound by in the UK by Pureprint

Author: Katie Foufouti
Illustrator: Nathalie Ortega (Beehive)
Series editor: Rebecca Adlard
Commissioning editor: Zoë Clarke
Publishing manager: Lisa Todd
Product managers: Jennifer Hall and Caroline Green
In-house editor: Alma Puts Keren
Project manager: Emily Hooton
Editor: Tessie Papadopoulou-Dalton
Proofreaders: Natalie Murray and Michael Lamb
Cover designer: Kevin Robbins
Typesetter: 2Hoots Publishing Services Ltd
Audio produced by id audio, London
Reading guide author: Emma Wilkinson
Production controller: Rachel Weaver
Printed and bound in the UK by Pureprint

Download the audio for this book and a reading guide for parents and teachers at www.collins.co.uk/839784